This
Nature Storybook
belongs to:

_____

_____

_____

WALKER BOOKS

For thousands of years,
fishermen have watched every autumn
as adult eels migrated down rivers into the sea,
and again every spring as the young eels returned.
But nobody knew what happened in between.
Where did the adults go to?
And where were the young eels born?
Today we think we know the secret of the eel,
but even now no one has ever seen a wild
eel lay eggs or an eel egg hatch.

For Martin Llewellyn
K. W.

For my Dad
M. B.

First published 1993 by Walker Books Ltd
87 Vauxhall Walk, London SE11 5HJ

This edition published 2008

10 9 8 7 6 5 4 3 2 1

Text © 1993 Karen Wallace
Illustrations © 1993 Mike Bostock

The right of Karen Wallace and Mike Bostock to be identified as
author and illustrator respectively of this work has been asserted by
them in accordance with the Copyright, Designs and Patents Act 1988

Printed in China

British Library Cataloguing in Publication Data:
a catalogue record for this book is available from the British Library

ISBN: 978-1-4063-1201-0

www.walkerbooks.co.uk

Think of an Eel

Karen Wallace

illustrated by

Mike Bostock

WALKER BOOKS
AND SUBSIDIARIES

LONDON • BOSTON • SYDNEY • AUCKLAND

Think of an eel.

He swims like a fish.

He slides like a snake.

There's a warm, weedy sea
to the south of Bermuda.
It's called the Sargasso.
No wind ever blows there,
no sailing ships sail there.
For thousands of years there
a secret lay hidden:
this salt, soupy sea
is where eels are born.
Deep down where it's blackest,
eel egg becomes eel.
He looks like a willow leaf,
clear as a crystal.

Baby eels are born in early spring.
A real one is only

about this big.

8

His fierce jutting mouth
has teeth like a sawblade.

He eats like a horse and
swims up through the water.

Young eels from the Sargasso travel either to Europe or to America — whichever their parents did before them.

Imagine this eel-leaf
and millions just like him
swimming on waves
across the wide sea.
Some are unlucky.
The seagulls are waiting.
Beaks snap like scissors
through wriggling water.

Eel swims for three years
till he reaches the shore

but the river's too cold, there's
still snow on the mountains.

Eels arrive in Europe around Christmas time. They wait offshore

So he waits in the water, turns into an elver.

Now he looks like a shoelace made out of glass.

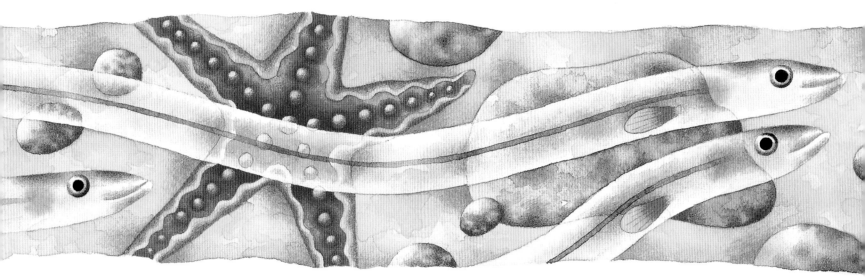

until spring, and as they wait they turn into elvers.

When spring
warms the shoreline,
the smell of fresh water
excites the glass elver.
Into the river
he swims like a mad thing.
He wriggles up rapids,
climbs rocks
around waterfalls.
River banks guide him.
Nothing will stop him.

Eels navigate by instinct.

They always seem to know where they are going.

Around a drowned oak stump,
through twisting green weeds,
a mudhole is hidden.

Mudholes, burrows and cracks in the
river bed are all homes for eels.

Eel knows without thinking
it's what he's been seeking.
He slips through the ooze.
This hole is his home.

In fresh water, the elvers grow bigger and turn into yellow eels.

Think of an eel.

After years in the river

he's slit-eyed and slimy

and thick like a snake.

He gulps stickleback eggs,

eats shrimps and small fishes.

shrimp

Eels feed mostly at night.

If the river is empty
he swims from the mudhole,
slips through the grass
to steal snails from the pond.

pond snail

An eel can live out of water for two days
or longer, if the ground is wet, breathing through its slimy skin.

One day eel stops eating.

His stomach is shrinking.

His long winding body

turns silver and black.

Eyes like blackcurrants

bulge into headlamps.

Now for the last time

eel slides from the mudhole.

His years in the river

are over for ever.

Silver eels usually leave the river in September or October.

Silver eel waits

for a night that is moonless,

when the rain from the mountains

has flooded the stream.

22

While they're waiting for a dark night, they sometimes get tangled up in a ball.

Then he slips
down the river, down to
the seashore. The time has arrived
for his long journey home.

For eighty days
silver eel swims through the ocean,
squirms like a secret
from seabird and sailor.

There are millions just like him,

deep down in the water,

swimming silently back

to the Sargasso Sea.

big eyes for seeing in the dark

There's eel-tomb and eel-cradle

in the weedy Sargasso.

After eighty days' swimming,

not eating, not sleeping,

eel's long, winding body

is worn out and wasted.

He spills the new life

carried deep in his belly,

then sinks through the sea

like a used silver wrapper.

The male eel's sperm fertilizes the female's eggs in the water.

Deep down where it's blackest,

eel egg becomes eel.

He looks like a willow leaf,

clear as a crystal.

His fierce jutting mouth

has teeth like a sawblade.

He eats like a horse and

swims up through the water.

Imagine this eel-leaf

and millions just like him

swimming on waves

across the wide sea…

Index

Look up the pages to find
out about all these eel things. Don't
forget to look at both kinds of words:
this kind *and this kind*.

A note from the author

Karen Wallace has always
been fascinated by eels.
"Their story is magical and
truly mysterious," she says.
"Even today, the spawning
grounds of some eel
species are still
unknown..."

A note from
the illustrator

Mike Bostock remembers
from his youth strange
myths about the origin of eels.
"They sprang from horse's tails
dipped in the river or from the mud of
the riverbed," he says. "Reading Karen's
text, I was captivated by the fact that
the eel had a life story as
extraordinary as those myths,
and I tried to put that feeling
into my pictures."

Praise for Nature Storybooks...

"For the child who constantly asks How? Why?
and What For? this series is excellent."
The Sunday Express

"A boon to parents seeking non-fiction picture books to read
with their children. They have excellent texts
and a very high standard of illustration to go with them."
The Daily Telegraph

"As books to engage and delight children, they work superbly.
I would certainly want a set in any primary
classroom I was working in."
Times Educational Supplement

"Here are books that stand out from the crowd,
each one real and individual in its own right and
the whole lot as different from most other series non-fiction
as tasty Lancashire is from processed Cheddar."
Books for Keeps

Find notes for teachers about how to use Nature Storybooks in the classroom at
www.walkerbooks.co.uk

Nature Storybooks support KS 1-2 Science